Claudine Glot

Brocéliande and its High Places

" History, legend and dizzy heights.
Three doors enabling one to enter into the legend and kingdom of Brocéliande.
" Philippe Le Guillou, *Brocéliande*.

Photographs: Yvon Boëlle

Translation: Padrig Koroller, Treiñ

ÉDITIONS OUEST-FRANCE
13, rue du Breil, Rennes

An inspired Landscape

Everyone can cross Paimpont forest, but how many will arrive at Brocéliande? Brocéliande does not exist in administrative cartography: it's a forest which is part of us and which one always hopes to encounter. "Forest of dreams and enchantment" said Albert Samain, General De Gaulle's favourite poet. A real forest, however, where one may loose oneself among outcrops of rock, deserted moors, clusters of oaks and the presence of waters.

As in one of these giddy knot works with which the Celts decorate their work, so the threads of nature, history and legend intertwine in Brocéliande; they combine, respond, and interweave to endlessly recreate the fascination of a sylvan universe of trees and armour.

Our imagination and the substance of our dreams take root in a landscape. In Brocéliande, legend is anchored to rock, water and trees.

Brocéliande with its rock base, six million years old: red slate, granite, quartz. An austere base which perforates the forest mantle in numerous places; the spine of a dragon dozing on the ridges of the Val sans Retour (Vale of no Return), gigantic claws held towards the village of Beauvais, a ruined castle which was never completed beside the meanderings of the Pont Dom Jean stream. There, where the forest became a quarry at La Moutte or La Marette, the still badly scarred wounds in the rock tell of the times of the Cyclops and the fire of the Earth.

Brocéliande of fresh and pure waters: springs, streams, especially lakes -nineteen at least- enamel the map with blue. Among the longest, the Pas-Du-Houx lake with its ninety hectares bordered to the west by the Brocéliande and Pas-Du-Houx castles ; that of Paimpont which laps against the walls of the old abbey ; that of Comper which masks the crystal

◁◁ ***At the edge of mystery (photo courtesy of Artus).***

▽ ***The Aff footbridge.***

palace of the faerie Vivian and behaves like an internal sea in strong wind. Also, the beautiful calm lakes of les Forges and Perray, which were formerly industrious, when iron working devoured the carpet of vegetation.

Brocéliande of trees finally; beeches, oaks, birches, chestnuts, alders, the first residents have only too often given way to conifers. Later and foreign, pines and firs were planted on the moors around 1830 to draw wealth from them.

The moors, cropped vegetation of gorse, broom and heather, is part of the bulk of the forest: medieval stories bear witness to it in which "lande" (moors) has been rhymed with Brocéliande.

The landscapes here are vested with the dreams of men. The fascination does not only come from the obscurity of the forest. It gives birth to marvellous beings who were perhaps divinities before being the heroes of romances, and who have inhabited the shadows from time immemorial. The knights, Yvain, Gawain or Lancelot, maintain strange contacts with the supernatural world, and demonstrate their out of the ordinary gifts. It happens that the faeries, Morgan, Vivian, Laudine, have very human sentiments. Also Merlin, spirit of the forest, plays the role of intercessor between man and nature, the human and the supernatural.

Brocéliande chateau.

Private property

Brocéliande is divided between the Basse Forêt (lower forest) to the east of Paimpont, and the Haute Forêt (upper forest) to the west. Ninety percent of its 7,000 hectares are private property. Only 600 hectares belong to the National Forestry Office. Forestry is largely practised throughout the bulk of the forest. That is why public access to part of the forest is forbidden throughout the year. Some of the footpaths are closed from the first of October to the first of April during the hunting season (stags, deer, wild boar, small game).

The Other World

Let us reflect at the threshold of Brocéliande, of the sense of the Other World, the Celtic concept of the supernatural world. A world of gods, faeries, spirits, including those of the dead, it is not situated in distant time and space. It duplicates our own world everywhere and always; it is interdependent and sometimes dependent on it. Its borders which often take the form of rivers or lakes, may do away with themselves. Brocéliande is part of the gateway to the Other World, through which man may have access to the supernatural.

Brocéliande and the birth of the romance

In the twelfth century, a new literary genre saw the light of day: books which did not seek to educate or enlighten, but to please, to distract by telling good stories. Accessible to all, they were written in the language of the people, Romance (the future French language), which gave its name to this type of writing.

Among the first romances, a collection dedicated to King Arthur and his knights enjoyed enormous success. First *Roman de Brut* (1155) by Robert Wace, a poet in the service of Aliénor d'Aquitaine, then, between 1160 and 1180, five romances by Chrétien de Troyes: *Erec et Enide*, *Cligès*, *Le chevalier de la charette*, *Le Chevalier au lion*, *Le conte du Graal*. The Arthurian legend was built upon these works and their successors. At the beginning of the thirteenth century, Jehan Bodel explained that three matters could be used to write a romance: that of France - epic poems such as the *Chanson de Roland*; that of Rome the great - ancient history, Greek or Latin; and that of Britain*. He added that both authors and public preferred the Matter of Britain* (Great Britain and Armorica) as the British* stories are so fantastic and seductive.

The academics, especially Jean Marx, have proved that the Arthurian legend indisputably comes from Celtic mythology. After their conversion to Christianity, the Celtic people preserved their primae-

* Translators footnote: Britain and British was (and still is in French) applied to both Brittany and Great Britain.

Merlin and Blaise.

The pathway to adventure.

val myths, while little by little forgetting their meaning. Despite the incertitudes of history, especially invasions, these Celtic legends were orally passed down for centuries on both sides of the Channel, particularly after the British emigration to Armorica in the fifth century. In Ireland, from the seventh century, the monks put into writing what remained of Irish Celtic mythology. Between Ireland, Wales, Brittany, France, Celtic legends were disseminated by bards, storytellers and minstrels. Collected by court poets in Wales, France, then in various courts throughout Europe, adapted according to the cultural and social components of the time, they provided the matter for the Arthurian romances. Brocéliande also then appeared in the books to fill our dreams with its procession of magic.

The Arthurian romance though, does not only follow on from Celtic mythology. Christian marvels, mediaeval symbolism, courtly culture of Occitania and Oriental influences are also mixed into it in different degrees.

But where is Brocéliande?

The identification of the forest of Paimpont with the legendary Brocéliande has been passionately debated in controversies as sterile as they are whimsical. Medieval charters and customs leave no doubt and call Brécilien,

The forest of apparitions (photo courtesy of Artus).

The gateway to the other world.

Bréchéliant, Brékilien or Brocéliande the totality or the heart of what is now the forest of Paimpont.

If proof be necessary for men of little faith, it can be summarised in the vigorous affirmation of Félix Bellamy: "That is the true Brocéliande, which contains Barenton ." One is tempted to add: the true Barenton, the fountain which according to the legend "boils whilst remaining cold" and which is flanked by a perron (stone slab) able to conjure up storms.

In the heart of our Brocéliande, the fountain of Barenton keeps watch. Nitrogen bubbles cross it to escape from the depth of the water and it looks like the surface of the water is starting to boil.

The creatures of the deep waters (photo, Amarok, courtesy of Lapica).

Galahad in combat with two knights.

Beside it, a large stone - Merlin's perron - is endowed with the power conjuring up a storm, if the ritual were known for doing it. In 1467, The Charter of Usage and Customs of the forest of Brocéliande, which determined the rights and duties of the owners and inhabitants of Brocéliande, stated that Guy de Laval, Lord of Comper, owned the fountain and only he could conjure up a storm. The heat wave of 1835 is often quoted when the clergy of Concoret held a procession to Barenton to make it rain. In 1954 again, the members of the Arthurian Congress proceeded with the ritual aspersion: the storm, faithful to the meeting, let fall its downpour on the members of the Congress, delighted by the persistence of the magic traditions.

The Centre of Arthurian Imaginary

This association created in Rennes in 1988, has been located since 1990, in the Château de Comper-en-Brocéliande thanks to its owners, M. and Mme Ferrand. The Arthurian Centre has, as its aim, to create quality cultural animation around all the themes relating to the forest of Brocéliande, the Subject of Bretagne and Celtic mythology. This covers research, literature, fine art, cinema and shows. The association organises exhibitions in the Château de Comper, guided tours in the forest of Brocéliande, conferences and shows during six months of the year.

The enchanted forests

Heir of the forest sanctuary of the Celts, the enchanted forest of the Arthurian romances represents more than just a simple decor. Scotland or Ireland, Darnantes or Northumberland forest, Calidan or Morois forest where Tristan and Isolt took refuge, Brocéliande sums them all up. It shelters the white animals, messengers from the Other World, the wild man, the lion and the serpent-dragon, the diabolic goblins...It contains magic waters, fountains, rivers or lakes. The knights come here to search for adventure. In the heart of the forest are some hermits who offer sound advice, and the ladies wait for love in the clearings.

Barenton fountain.

Iron and the forest

The Lower Forest or industrialised forest still retains the marks of the metal-working industry. The ground is rich in iron ore. The purple slate with rusted faults indicates as much, like the ferrous oxide which reddens the streams. The working of iron is very old in Brocéliande. We have known, for a long time, of the existence of monastic forges from the thirteenth century and of an arms factory in the village of Gué, in Plélan in the 15th century. Recent excavations have revealed traces of metalworking activity from the first or second century before Christ. But the Forges of Paimpont were really created in 1653 by François d'Andigné and Jacques de Farcy. The forest provided the ore, the wood for making charcoal for the furnaces, and water, the source of energy for moving the bellows, the hammers and all the rolling mills. For a little more than two centuries, the working of iron made up the main part of the economic activity of Brocéliande. The iron, of excellent quality, was used for domestic products, civil engineering and naval armaments. Modernised around 1820, the Forges reached their peak in 1853. Short lived triumph: the decline began in 1857, Brittany could not compete with the North, the East or the United Kingdom. The blast furnaces went out in 1884. In the village of Les Forges, there remains today the house of the forge master, some workers' cottages, a collection of very run down blast furnaces, a foundry and rolling

The ironworks in operation.

A soil rich in iron.

The Hindrés oak.

mills (private property). By the side of the road still stand two chapels dedicated to St Eloi and the former office of the watchman.

Because of the enormous quantity of wood consumed and the planning of the hydrographic network, industry has moulded the current appearance of Brocéliande. Little mature timber, lots of coppices. Some trees were spared the axe: Arthur's oak at Comper, the majestic oak of the Hindrés in the lower forest, the Rues Eon oak in Concoret which, it is said, sheltered during the revolution - with the aid of the Virgin Mary - the evasive priest Guillotin, the Gelée beech, that of Ponthus, and the marvellous ancestor, the beech of Rocheplate.

Les Forges lake (photo courtesy of Artus).

The tree and the Celtic forest

Rare are the civilisations which have not constructed temples to the glory of their gods. The Celts are singular in this respect because of an alternative concept of a holy place. As wrote Christian-J. Guyonvarc'h, "the only unique sanctuary is the dense and living forest which at the dawn of history covered immense stretches of north and west Europe. Our Brocéliande is the last shred of this ancient splendour". For the true divine principle is the tree," symbol and support of the sacred" and the forest is nothing "but a repetition and multiplication of the cosmic tree".

Our Lady of Paimpont (photo courtesy of Artus).

The creatures of the night

The night brings with it a worrying procession throughout. The washer-women of the night, who beat their washing in the Val sans Retour and drown the imprudent passer-by in the Rauco, are found elsewhere in Brittany. On the other hand, Belle Jeanette only haunts the triangular fields of Brocéliande at nightfall. Does she appear as a cat, a dog or an eagle owl? The three at once no doubt. As soon as her golden eyes dart onto the passer-by, you must hasten to greet her by saying clearly "Good evening Belle Jeanette", if not she tears the imprudent person from the ground, carries him far away and leaves him alone, without memory... for some days at least.

St. Judicaël's hand reliquary.

Prehistory and legend

Paimpont abbey

History tells us that Paimpont was founded in the 7th century by Judicaël, King of Dumnonia. At the beginning of the 10th century the Vikings cleared away its first buildings. The abbey church, built in the 13th century on an 11th century base, was largely renovated in the 15th century. The large accommodation building was built in the 17th century. The beautiful woodwork that decorates the nave, the pulpit and a sacristy of the abbey church also date from this period. A statue of Our Lady of Paimpont from the 15th century is still highly venerated today - is this the statue miraculously hidden in Rennes during the wars of the Ligue? Two other 15th century statues represent St Méen and St Judicaël. The sacristy of the abbey church contains a treasure, the main pieces of which are a reliquary hand of St Judicaël in gold plated silver and an ivory Christ. The reliquary was offered to the abbey by the mother of Anne of Brittany. The ivory Christ, sculpted in the 18th century is moving because of the mixture of pain and calm which can be read on the tortured face. Paimpont abbey, occupied by the Benedictines then by the Augustines, was handed over to secular clergy and the civil administration in 1791. Facing the abbey, on the north bank of the lake, a replica of the Lourdes grotto, surrounded by small streams, trees and flowers, was made with slag (residue of the iron smelting process). A statue of St Judicaël faces it.

Legendary megaliths

More than fifty funeral mounds, gallery graves, cists, menhirs, and alignments were erected in Brocéliande from the Neolithic Age (3000 - 2500 BC), to the Bronze Age (2000 BC). The main monuments, excavated between 1982 and

Paimpont abbey.

One of the three Trébran rocks in Concoret.

1985 by a CNRS (National Centre for Scientific Research) team under the direction of Jacques Briard, yielded precious clues to the forest's past.

Did the tribes, which succeeded one another on this land, consider it as a sacred place to bury their dead and honour their gods? Did the mythical aura of Brocéliande dawn five thousand years ago?

The Giants' Tomb in Campénéac, a large Bronze Age cist (3 m x 2 m), built with the menhirs from a destroyed alignment, also reminds us of that legendary presence. The encounter or fight with the giants was part of the initiation into the Arthurian knighthood. Even if the wild man that Calogrenant then Yvain met on the way to Barenton was an easy going giant, the Black Knight,

The Monks garden (photo courtesy of Artus).

As a legendary princess (photo courtesy of Artus).

Barenton's guardian, demanded a fight to the death. The young King Arthur had to face the cruel giant of St Michael's Mount who had abducted and assaulted Princess Helen. The Giant's Tomb is also called the Old Woman's Rock. Perhaps in memory of an enchantress, a divinity honoured here? When the origins grow more distant the great and beautiful supernatural beings sometimes become old and counterfeit.

For a long time, country people summoned faeries, giants, enchanters along with the builders. The Three Rocks of Trébran, in Concoret also fell from the apron of a faerie who was carrying them towards St Michael's Mount then under construction. No explanation has ever been suggested for the presence of these three enormous blocks of roughly hewn pudding-stone: we have to be content with this one.

One of the most enigmatic monuments of the forest, the Monks' Garden, is a 27 m long quadrilateral formed with alternate blocks of red slate and white

Gurwan moors.

pudding-stone (whose deposit is more than 3 km away, near Tréhorenteuc). Erected about three thousand years B.C., it was reused at the beginning of the Bronze age. No explanation has been found for this original construction. The excavations yielded few artefacts and no bones, as the acidity of the soil destroyed them. Popular tradition sees in it the expression of divine anger against Lord Gastern de Tréhorenteuc. Soldier and miscreant, he took a monk hostage and decided - sacrilege! - to hunt on All Souls' Day. During vespers, a terrible storm broke on the moor where he was riding. The calm having returned, the inhabitants of the village headed for the moors and discovered that the entire hunt had been turned to stone: one of the variants of the theme of the damned hunter.

Vivian's Hotié.

The Butte aux Tombes

The moors surrounding the Monks' Garden is called the Butte aux Tombes (Knoll of Graves). It is strewn with small, low graves, perhaps the remains of a Neolithic cemetery. Everything here evokes the passage into the Other World. Doctor Alphonse Guérin, inventor of the wadded plaster, was no doubt sensitive to the melancholy and the feeling of eternity that emanates from these moors, when he decided to build the mausoleum there, in which he has lain since 1895.

△ *Merlin as a stag.*

Merlin's tomb.

The faeries' hawthorn.

Original monuments

Local tradition has enriched the megalithic monuments with the memory of the Arthurian legends. Vivian's Hotié (house), or the Tomb of the Druids is a Neolithic cist oriented east- west, surrounded by a double, circular, stone facing. The excavations yielded some axes, pearls, shards of pottery and fragments of millstones. The axes are in Plussulien dolerite (Côtes d'Armor). The fragment of millstone indicates the evolution of the society: We can not yet talk about agriculture, but hunting was no longer the sole means of finding food. The analysis of the fossilised pollen found beneath the monument give a glimpse of the vegetation of five thousand years ago: sparse forest, or abundant ashes, limes and hazels, with curiously few oaks.

The Tomb of Merlin is all that remains of a Neolithic gallery grave. A photograph of 1892 shows it in very bad condition, but imposing, with a dozen slabs still standing. Two years later, it was destroyed by the landowner. Perhaps because of the usual legend of a crock of

gold buried under the megalith? Or because of the fear of these unexplained monuments?

The Tomb of Merlin shares with the Barenton fountain the privilege of having remained, or having become again, a place of worship across time. One could pass these two red slate blocks, overlooked by a very old holly, if one's attention was not drawn by the profusion of wreathes, flowers and humble objects left there. Nothing spectacular: here the truly inner pathway proceeds from the forest force, the spiritual presence and the memory of time. Symbolic trees - the oak of wisdom, the holly of eternity, the hawthorn of the faeries - cast a shadow on the tomb.

Following double page: ***Perceval encounters an enchantress in the forest. (D.R.)***

Comper and Vivian's lake.

All around, hope and expectation are manifested: wishes, small offerings to the Enchanter, to tell him that we believe in him, we need his help and we are waiting for him. Some, fearing that the years may blunt Merlin's capacities, clarify their greetings in writing (have they forgotten that Merlin did not write and had his story composed by his old master Blaise?). Others practise the ritual of the seven times knotted hair. Some sleep there accompanied with a cat, a great telluric power detector. Sometimes people come here in the middle of the night to commune with the spirit of the forest and to pray for Merlin to intercede for the trees...

Very close to Merlin's tomb, is the fountain of Youth which some people insist on visiting. It is not one of the most enchanting places, and it would be better to penetrate deeper into the woods towards the Pont Dom Jean, the most secret of the lakes of Brocéliande, where, in autumn, the stag comes to bell. Pont Dom Jean, with its still waters, its enormous oaks and its red rocks, waits for the visit of the faerie-knights who cross the lakes to win the hearts of the forlorn queens and to father prodigious sons. On dark days, it evokes perilous waters, such as those crossed by Lancelot on the Bridge of the Sword to deliver Guenevere.

Merlin

Born of the Devil and a woman, Merlin comes into the world with disturbing powers which he used for the good: he knows the past and the future, sees that which is hidden, moves at infinite speed and may take on any appearance. Neither man nor god, but counsellor, soothsayer, magician, prophet, Merlin teaches King Arthur how to unite and govern his country. He plays the same role that was played by the druid towards the king in the Celtic kingdoms. It is on his instructions, that the king founds the Round Table and announces the quest for the Holy Grail. Merlin is not a courtier, his true domain is the forest, to which he retires regularly to meditate, work, and understand the visible and invisible world.

Merlin and Vivian in Brocéliande

If faeries are the ladies of the Other World, then surely Vivian is a faerie. Her father, King Dionas was the goddess Diana's godchild and Vivian, from her childhood, was pledged to the forest of Brocéliande, which she covers endlessly. She was instructed in the sciences of the plants and the stars. When, at the beginning of her fifteenth year she meets Merlin near Barenton, she is fascinated by his knowledge and mystery. He takes her as his pupil because he loves her and she has the same nature as him. Their relations are those of two people in love, perhaps two lovers, and especially those of two initiates speaking the same language.

At Comper, in the valley which stretches in front of the old fortified castle of Dionas, Merlin built a marvellous crystal palace for Vivian; so that she would not be bothered by people gazing upon her, he masked its appearance, in a semblance of a lake. An illusion so troubling that still today, in front of the lake, some people, persuaded by the reality of what they see, sometimes forget the crystal castle. It is true that those who Vivian, the Lady of the Lake, allows to glimpse, even for an instant, the reflection of her domain, are rare...

Many years after the meeting of the faerie and the enchanter, King Ban of Benoïc and Queen Helen, fleeing their

Comper castle

Comper was perhaps one of the castles of Salomon, king of Brittany, but his history begins with Raoul de Gaël, companion of William the Conqueror at Hastings. From the 13th century, Comper became one of the principle fortified places of upper Brittany. During the Breton War of Succession, it was ravaged by du Guesclin and rebuilt in 1375. In 1467, Guy de Laval had The Charter of Usage and Customs of the forest of Brocéliande written there. In the 16th century, it was passed to the Rieux family, then to the Coligny family. In 1595, during the Wars of the Ligue, the Duke of Mercoeur's troops seized Comper and survived a several months long siege. In reprisal, Henry IVth had the outer wall dismantled in 1598. In 1860, Armand de Charette rebuilt the central building destroyed by fire in 1790.

The Lady of the Lake carries off Lancelot.

▷▷ *Arthurian chivalry (Amarok).*

kingdom which had been invaded by King Claudas of the desert Land, arrived in Brocéliande. The king died of sorrow and exhaustion. The queen, had the pain of seeing her young son dragged under the water of a magnificent lake by a lady dressed in white. How could Queen Helen have guessed that this lady was Vivian and that the lake did not exist? In despair, she retired to a convent. The Lady of the Lake brought up the young boy as her son. She taught him the Sciences and the Arts and weaponry and she taught him the spirit of chivalry. When Lancelot reached his fifteenth year, Vivian told him that he must leave the enchanted domain and become a knight of the Round Table. Cruel separation. Lancelot arrives at the court of Arthur completely dressed in white, radiantly handsome, haloed by his faerie childhood. In spite of his youth, he revealed himself to be the best of the knights. For his good and bad fortune, he fell in love with Guenevere, the wife of King Arthur.

If Vivian offered the Knight to the world of humans, she took back from it the Enchanter. To keep the vagabond of the forest and the royal courts near to her, she looks for the most dangerous of his spells, that which enables him to imprison, without bars, wall or chains, he around whom it is chanted. Merlin had guessed a long time ago the desire of Vivian when, one day in May, after a long wander in the forest, he confided to her the nine sentences of the enchantment. He knows that the days of the Round Table are numbered, that the Quest for the Holy Grail is announced, that after the last battle, Arthur will disappear from the eyes of man for centuries and centuries. Then Merlin chooses to allow himself to be imprisoned by his dearly beloved in Brocéliande and to live there, invisible but present, in communion with the trees, the animals and the stars. Merlin and Vivian are truly in Brocéliande; but who has eyes to see them?

Excalibur.

The knight of the Round Table

Their valour only makes the knights worthy of belonging to the brotherhood of the Round Table. Their number varies from 12 to 1600: Lancelot, Yvain, Gawain, Perceval and Galahad are among the most famous. They seek adventure alone for their honour, the service of their Lady or the King or God. They have a moral obligation to "keep to the path of righteousness" and show themselves to be courteous. Their life is shared between their time at court with the festivals, the tournaments, the relating of adventures, and their time of roaming. The path of the knight passes through the forest, as it is there that he proves his courage, faced with the marvels that it holds and the terrors that it creates. Arthurian chivalry was accomplished in the Quest of the Holy Grail that, however, marks the break up and the end of the Round Table.

Joust in the heart of Brocéliande (photo courtesy of Polater).

Barenton

Barenton epitomises Brocéliande. In order to find the fountain, you must venture into the heart of the forest, sometimes getting lost, as the path of the quest is anything but straight. You must also marvel that such a simple fountain has crossed time and the dreams of men, and moved people with the fervour that it still engenders today.

The *Knight with the lion*, the romance in which Chrétien de Troyes tells the story of Yvain, the nephew of King Arthur is set around Barenton. A young knight, Yvain leaves the court for Brocéliande where he knows he will meet with adventure near to a fountain with strange powers. In the forest, he meets the wild man who puts him on the path to Barenton. Yvain pours water from the fountain onto the perron. An incredible storm breaks; the calm returns and a black knight suddenly appears who challenges Yvain to mortal combat. The latter, mortally wounds his adversary and pursues him to his castle where he receives the help of Luned, a follower of Laudine, Lady of the Fountain and widow of the black Knight. He falls in love with Laudine and, with the help of Luned, marries her. After their marriage the Lady of the Fountain grants him a year of freedom, but he forgets to return on time and she banishes him. He wanders around Brocéliande for months then, to win back his wife, he passes through the hardest of trials: hunger, solitude, madness. Accustomed to only serving his own glory, he learns to fight and suffer for others. At the end of

Yvain, the lion and the dragon.

his wanderings in the forest, during which he saves a marvellous lion which becomes attached to him, he wins back the heart of his lady and becomes the guardian of the fountain.

To get to Barenton, you pass through the hamlet of Folle-Pensée: a more or less convincing etymology contends that the name signifies "madness cured". This explanation refers to a druidic school of medicine established in Barenton which had as its speciality, the cure of mental disorders. A hypothesis which is as difficult to support as it is to refute. That the druids were remarkable doctors is true, that Brocéliande housed a druidic college is not unlikely, that the waters of Brocéliande had curative properties, we still await the proof. So, let us remain on the fringes of the probable and ask for the testimony of Arthurian literature: Tristan, Lancelot, Yvain and even Merlin himself confront the ordeal of madness. They seek refuge, alone and naked, in the heart of the forest, near the soothing fountains and are reborn in this return to the wild state.

Merlin.

The Errant Knight.

Trécesson

the Lady and the Lake (photo courtesy of Artus).

Trécesson, the most beautiful of the castles of Brocéliande, is surrounded with ghostly legends. The most famous tells of the misfortunes of the bride of Trécesson. One night, a poacher hidden in the castle grounds, sees a dark coach stop near to him. Two men in black get out and begin digging a deep hole. The work having been finished, they take a young woman in a wedding dress from the coach and, despite her tears, bury her alive before making their getaway. The poacher informs M. de Trécesson who gives the order for the young woman to be immediately delivered. But, the help arrives too late and, at daybreak, the poor soul passes away without revealing her secret. All of the investigations were in vain; the bride's terrible secret was never discovered. The veil and the headdress remained on the altar of the castle chapel until the revolution. Touching these relics was supposed to procure a husband for young girls. It is said at Campénéac, Augan and around, that on certain nights, the ghost of the poor soul comes back and floats around the moat, forever the White Lady of Trécesson.

Built in the 15th century by Jean de Trécesson, the castle remained in the hands of his family until 1773. Its history is more serene than its legend. During the wars of the Ligue, Mercoeur's troops, who ravaged the region, spared Trécesson. During the Terror a member of the girondin Convention hid there for a year. From 1849 to 1870 the castle became a farm-school. It is now the home of the Count of Prunelé.

The wars of the Ligue

The Sainte Ligue (holy league), or Saint Union was formed in 1568 by Henri de Guise, with the aim of defending the Catholic church against the Huguenots. It also supported the Guises against the Valois for the possession of the throne of France. In Brittany certain important families rallied to the Protestant cause, among them were the Rohans and the Lavals, rulers of Brocéliande. The Duke of Mercoeur, Governor of Brittany, took command of the Ligue's troops, as much for his attachment to Catholicism as for his personal ambition. Under his government, Brittany was ravaged by a civil war, aggravated by assorted acts of banditry. The troubles of the Ligue were calmed by the conversion to Catholicism of Henri IV and finished in 1598 by the promulgation of the edict of Nantes.

The chapel and the Lady of Trécesson.

Above Trécesson are spread the Tiot mounds which house Neolithic graves. On these moors are the chapel of St. John and the ruins of a small hermitage built by the Hospitallers of St. John. The chapel contains the tomb of M. de Sivry, Lord of Trécesson at the beginning of the 19th century. Behind the Tiot mounds the public footpath leads to the Giant's Tomb, Vivian's Hotié and the Val sans Retour. It passes in front of a curious, very weathered cross, the Lucas cross, which commemorates the place where, in 876 the murderers of King Salomon (Salaün) of Brittany, Pascweten, the Count of Vannes and Gurwan, the Count of Rennes, confronted one another. Is it a local myth or historical fact? In the land of Brocéliande history and legend easily exchange their prerogatives...

Trécesson castle.

Tréhorenteuc

Whoever enters Tréhorenteuc church is amazed by the paintings, stained glass, mosaics and pavings which celebrate the fusion of the Christian faith with the Celtic tradition and the Arthurian legends. For Henri Gillard, the sanctuary's master craftsman, they all belong to the same faith. Christianity here succeeded the religion of the druids, and the Arthurian legends were written into this continuity. What he made of his church did not only concern the aesthetic, but also a symbolic language which had been forged from diverse traditions.

St. John's chapel.

Some examples? The symbolics of colours: violet, colour of harmony, dyes the cloak of Jesus and the aquilegia flower in the large mosaic. The Celtic domain is indicated by oaks and acorns in the large stained glass window, the triskelia on the railings of St. Eutrope's chapel, a boar's head on St. Onenne's table. Christian symbols mix with Celtic themes: fish, crosses, alpha and omega and the emblematic animals of the apostles.

The representation of the legends of Brocéliande and of the Holy Grail are

Reverend Gillard

Reverend Henri Gillard arrived in Tréhorenteuc in 1942: the villagers, isolated in the forest of Paimpont were not an exemplary congregation. The reverend undertook to revive the parish community and to restore the church. Very sensitive to the spirit of Brocéliande and to the legends of the Round Table, he did not see the opposition between the Word that he should have been teaching and the Celtic myths. The Christianized legend of the Holy Grail became his ideal. From 1942 to 1954, he undertook works which made of "a place of worship a place of culture". He sought without respite, individual or collective donations. He published from 1948 guides dedicated to Tréhorenteuc and Brocéliande. The curious flooded in. The fame of the church grew greater. Too great perhaps. In 1962, Reverend Gillard had to leave Tréhorenteuc. He returned as a visitor from 1968 onwards. His body has rested in his church of the Holy Grail since 1979.

Eon of the Star

From 1145 to 1148, Eon of the Star led the life of an illuminated monk-bandit near Barenton, pillaging monasteries and manors with his companions in poverty. He proclaimed himself son of God, Great Judge of the living and the dead. Heretic to some, magicians to others, some considered him to be the last druid of Brocéliande. His influence and his exactions caused him to appear before the council of Rheims. His inflammatory declarations appeared to the ecclesiastical tribunal to be more related to mental derangement than to heresy: it was even supposed that Merlin had breathed into him a little of his madness. He escaped the stake but not the prison, where he died shortly afterwards. His disciples were pursued and the "eonite" heresy disappeared.

The Holy Grail window at Tréhorenteuc.

the main originality of the church. They even occupy the Pathway of the Cross, painted by Karl Rezabeck, a German prisoner of war under the orders of the reverend Gillard who wanted twelve of the stations to represent Tréhorenteuc and its surroundings. He even had Jesus represented falling at the feet of Morgan the faerie, the incarnation of lust. Such an improper presence that it earns the reverend some severe admonitions.

Four paintings decorate the choir. The first represents the family of St. Onenne, the sister of King Judicaël: she had made a vow of poverty and looked after the geese at Tréhorenteuc. The stain glass windows of the nave tell of her life and her miracles. On the second painting, Morgan can be found again facing Lancelot in the middle of the enchantments of the Val sans Retour. The third has Barenton in its centre: Yvain and the Black Knight, Vivian enchanting Merlin, Eon of the Star in his handsome stolen clothes and Ponthus fighting for Sidoine can be seen in it. The last one represents the nourishing Holy Grail appearing to the Knights of the Round Table.

The three stained glass windows of the choir sum up the legend of the Holy Grail, shown first of all as a simple goblet, dark green, on the table of the Last Supper. In the central window, the Holy Grail, having become miraculous by receiving the blood of the crucified, shines on Joseph of Arimathea imprisoned for having offered his tomb to Christ. Christ resuscitated stands in front of the prisoner.

The white stag mosaic at Tréhorenteuc.

The omega mosaic.

The Holy Grail from the film " Excalibur " (photo courtesy of Artus).

The Holy Grail

The Holy Grail appears in 1180 in a romance of Chrétien de Troyes, Le Conte du Graal (The Story of the Holy Grail). The author does not reveal the nature of the mysterious object. Around 1200, Robert de Boron makes it the goblet of the Last Supper, into which Joseph of Arimathia collects the blood of Christ. According to Wolfram von Eschenbach, it is an enormous precious stone which had fallen from the sky. Whatever it is, the Holy Grail is always the source of blessing: it gives nourishment, life and immortality. Solid arguments defend the Celtic origin of this talisman. The Middle Ages made a Christian myth of the Holy Grail but the Church has never integrated it as its own. It has been the object of numerous interpretations, the most diverse movements have drawn inspiration from it, but who can say what it is? Perhaps "the spark of grace that divinity casts into each one of us, the desire for heaven, the infinite..."

Ponthus and Sidoine

Written in the 15th century, the *Romance of Ponthus* is the last mediaeval romance set in Brocéliande. Ponthus, son of the king, flees from Galicia to escape the Mohammedans. After a shipwreck on the Breton coast, he meets Sidoine, daughter of the king of Vannes, and the two fall in love. Ponthus becomes Constable of Little Brittany, but slanders separate the lovers. Ponthus takes refuge in Brocéliande and, to win back Sidoine, challenges the best knights to a tournament at the Fountain of Marvels (Barenton). Every Tuesday for one year, he defeats one of his adversaries and sends him as a prisoner to his dearly beloved. They get engaged but seven years passed by again before their love triumphed over all of the treachery. One doubtful etymology derives the name of Paimpont from that of Ponthus (Pen-Ponthi, capital of Ponthus). It is claimed that he lived near an oak which bears his name, in a castle destroyed long ago...

On the third window, the Knights of the Round Table assembled around the king have in turn a vision of the Holy Grail.

Each detail of the large mosaic, the work of Jean Delpech, was required by Reverend Gillard: a white stag with a golden collar surrounded by four red lions stand out from the stylized decor of the fountain of Barenton. The stag incarnates Christ and the lions represent the Apostles. Lancelot and his son Galahad had that vision, one as a warning against his love for the queen, the other to announce that he was on the path to the Holy Grail.

In the narthex, a fish tail and a ram's head flank the baptismal fonts, symbolising the alpha and the omega, next to the golden number, the guarantor of harmony. Then, the short sentence painted above the chapitret (south porch), the door is on the inside, is the final advice of the reverend Gillard to those in quest of the Holy Grail.

The Val sans retour

Notched deeply into the red slate, the Val always loses its visitors in the maze of its valleys. It is claimed that the fault in it is of iron ore which drives wild compasses and ghosts... but is it really certain?

If the deep waters of Comper summon the presence of Vivian, this beautiful, violent Val suits Morgan, the fearsome half-sister of King Arthur. She established herself there to exercise the sciences learned from Merlin and accommodate her sometimes ephemeral passions. Betrayed by one of her lovers, wounded in her love and in her pride, she avenged herself by turning the guilty parties into stone: they became the Rock of the Faux-Amants (false lovers) which dominates the valley. Then she enchanted the Val: faithful lovers may cross it without risk, but all unfaithful ones remain there, prisoners of an invisible wall of air. Once in the power of Morgan, they lose all notion of time: thinking to spend several days there, they remain there for months or for years. Blind to reality, they believe that they are living in a place dedicated to pleasure. That might have lasted for ever if Lancelot had not passed through there. Morgan could not imprison him as he avowed a perfect love of Guenevere. She attempted to fight him but none of the terrifying apparitions which she launched against him exhausted his courage. He broke the enchantment of the Val and Morgan had to give up her prisoners.

At the entrance to the Val sans retour, the Miroir-aux-Fees (faerie mirror) pool highlights the faerie influence on this valley. Everyone knows, since Alice in Wonderland, that there is a completely different world beyond the mirror. Through the Miroir-aux-Fees, you pass through the doorway of legends. Yet another sign, on top of the Val, a rock formation bears the name of Merlin's Seat as he had the habit of coming to watch the sun set over the forest, and to think of a thousand ways of enchanting the world there.

The ghosts are aware, when the occasion arises, of how to come to terms with men: they lived happily together with the millers of the Val mill, the ruins of which can be seen against the dam of the Miroir-aux-Fees. Four ponds fed the mill. The Miroir-aux-Fees has survived; to the west of the Val, the fourth pond was refilled with water by the Association for the Protection of the Val sans retour. By following the Rauco, the disembowelled dams of the other two ponds can be seen.

The Thanksgiving window.

The Golden Tree

In September 1990, the Val sans retour burned for five

The Valley of No Return (photo courtesy of Artus).

days. After the fire donations flowed in and the Association for the Protection of the Val sans retour orchestrated the clean up, the replantation and the protection of the disaster area. In memory of these events and to remember the necessity of the forest of legends, François Davin created the Gold of Brocéliande often called the Golden Tree. This gold leafed chestnut tree (90 grams of gold cover it), surrounded by five black trees carries a message. The black trees symbolise the burned forest and all of the forests destroyed by negligence or for profit. Gold, an inalterable metal, is traditionally associated with immortality. Covered with gold, a tree becomes eternal but this can only be the work of man. It is the same for the eternity of the forest. Otherwise only black trees will remain and a memory of beauty.

The purple countryside: red slate and foxgloves.

Gold in Brocéliande

Gold is not an unexpected metal in Brocéliande. The streams of Brocéliande and the Aff still carry today specks of this precious metal. A golden goblet, decorated with Celtic designs was discovered at the end of the last century in Brocéliande. One of the popular tales of the forest tells of the adventures of a little charcoal burner and a golden log.

The Golden Tree has become the new legend of Brocéliande. François Davin wanted it to evoke the head and antlers of a stag. The great stag of the old religions, the ferrier of souls to the eternal shores. The stag of legends, guiding the knights to adventure, the enchantment of the forest and the love of Ladies from the Other World. The Christic stag with the golden collar. Finally the white-footed stag into which Merlin liked to transform himself to haunt the woods and sometimes the palaces.

Gold, tree, stag... Merlin or Vivian, golden armour and antlers of leaves, powers of the forest. In the depth of a disenchanted time, Brocéliande, through the labyrinths of its valleys, its waters and its woods, opens to the soul the gates of the Great Time. That which will render you eternal...

The Aff valley

The wild heart of the old Brocéliande still survives in the Aff valley. Deeply embanked valley, dense vegetation where the forest atmosphere becomes fascinating. It is neither the domesticated forest of the Basse Forêt paths nor the moors or conifers of the Haute Forêt, but the deep and romantic forest where the echo of legendary times resonates. From the top of the Casse-Cou (Dare-Devil) rock, the revelation of the sweep of the forest can be had ; there, under a springtime setting sun, the forest offers one of its most fascinating faces. In 1993 and 1994, a dam threatened to swallow up the Aff valley: ten of thousands of the forest faithful stood up with a single watchword: no one shall touch Brocéliande!

◁ *The Faeries' mirror.*

◁ *Le Rauco.*

Bibliography

The Arthurian legend
Children
Les Chevaliers de la Table Ronde, Casterman.
Yvain, le chevalier au lion, *Lancelot, le chevalier à la charette*, *Perceval, Le conte du Graal*, by Chrétien de Troyes, Folio Junior, special publishing.

Adults
La Légende arthurienne, Bouquins.
Oeuvres complètes de Chrétien de Troyes, La Pléiade or la Pochotèque.
Lancelot en prose, Le Livre de Poche.
La Mort du roi Arthur, Champion.
Le Morte Darthur, Malory, L'Atalante.

Celtic studies
Research
La Civilisation celtique, Christian-J. Guyonvarc'h, Ouest-France.
La Société celtique, Christian-J. Guyonvarc'h, Ouest-France.
Les Druides, Christian-J. Guyonvarc'h, Ouest-France.
Les Fêtes celtiques, Christian-J. Guyonvarc'h, Ouest-France.

Studies
Les Guerriers de Finn, Michel Cazenave, Artus.
Le Gant de verre, le mythe de Tristan et Yseut, Philippe Walter, Artus.
Aux vents des royaumes, Michel Le Bris, Arthus.
Immortels, Merlin et Viviane, Philippe Le Guilloux, Arthus.
Le Testament de Merlin, Théophile Briant.

Stories, theatre
Livres des guerriers d'or, Philippe Le Guilloux, Gallimard.
The Ladies of the Lake, the Mists of Avalon, Marion Zimmer Bradley, Pygmalion and Le Livre de Poche.
Merlin, Michel Rio, Le Seuil.
Le Roi Pêcheur, Julien Gracq, Corti.
L'Enchanteur, René Barjavel, Denoël.

It is possible to get a more detailed bibliography on simple request at the Centre de l'Imaginaire arthurien (Centre for Arthurian Imaginary).

Practical information

Tréhorenteuc Tourist Office, 56430 Tréhorenteuc. Tel. 97 93 05 12.
Paimpont Tourist Information, 35380 Paimpont.

Pays d'Accueil de Brocéliande, rue de la Libération, 35380 Plélan-le Grand.
Pays d'accueil de la Table ronde, 7, rue du Val, 56800 Ploërmel. Tel. 97 73 33 33

Environment, forest care
Association de Sauvegarde du Val sans retour (Vale of no Return Preservation Association), Mairie de Ploërmel, 56800 Ploërmel. Tel. 97 73 20 73.
SOS Brocéliande, Le Pont de la Lande, 35380 Beignon.

Documentation on the legends of the Round Table and on Brocéliande forest, guided tours, books, etc. Centre de l'Imaginaire arthurien, Comper-en-Brocéliande Castle, 56800 Ploërmel. Tel. 97 22 79 96 - Fax 99 08 53 05.

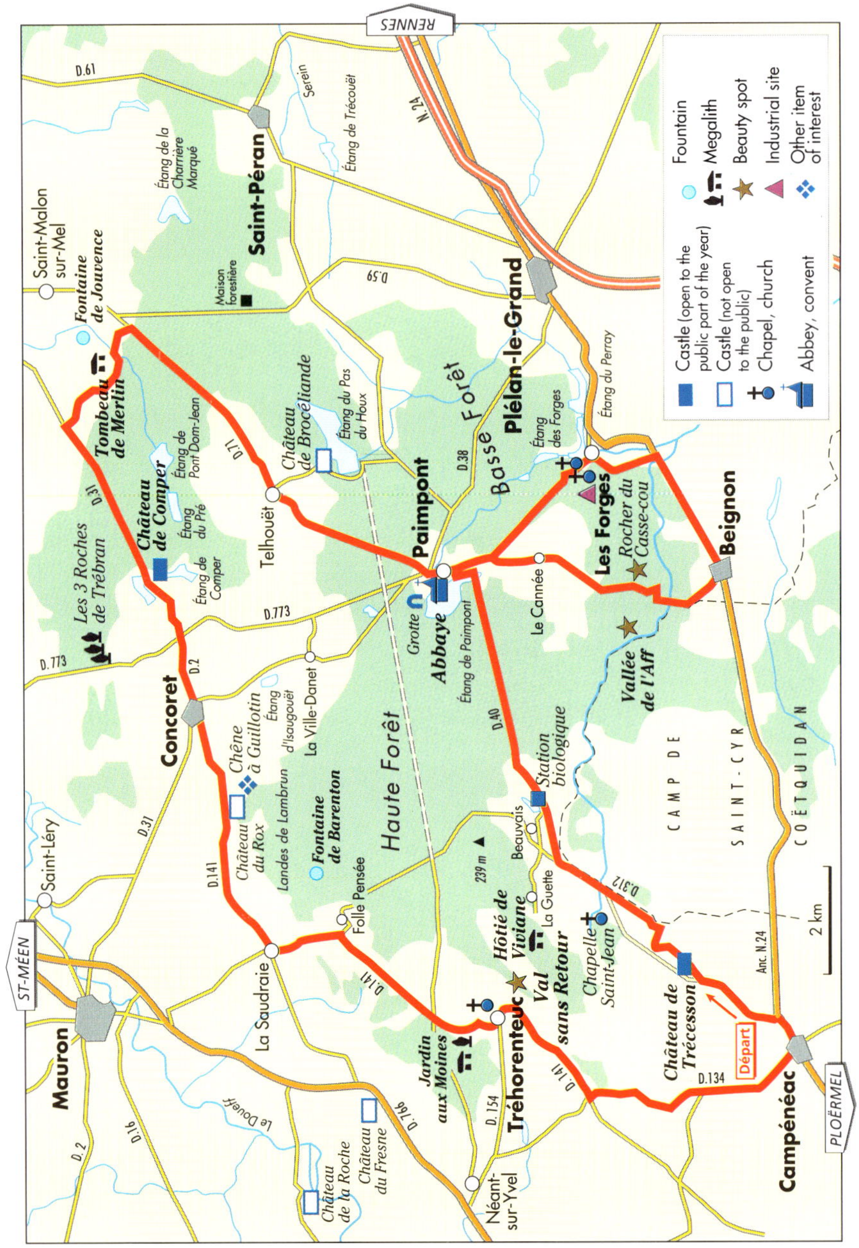

Front cover: **Trécesson castle**

Insert: **The Erran[t] Knight (detail)**

Back cover: **The gateway to the Other World**

Cartography: AFDEC, Paris

I.S.B.N. : 2.7373.2081.X - Dépôt légal : mars 1996 - N° d'éditeur : 3470.02.06.01.01
Technic Plus Impression, Betton (35)